"I am so glad to see these passionate, timely, thoughtful, and pastoral expositions in print. They will have done much good when first preached, and will do yet more good now they are available in book form. I hope they will have a wide readership."

Christopher Ash
Writer-in-Residence,
Tyndale House

"Living by faith is never easy, especially in the midst of a global pandemic. Thankfully, the Bible gives us examples of men and women who stood firm in their faith through difficult days. In *Living by Faith in Turbulent Times*, Jonathan Griffiths takes us to the Bible's 'Hall of Faith' to show us what living by faith looks like in practical terms. Griffiths presents God's timeless truth in a timely way. Your faith will be strengthened and stretched as you read!"

Rick Reed
President,
Heritage College and Seminary

Living by Faith in Turbulent Times

LIVING
by
FAITH
in turbulent times

JONATHAN GRIFFITHS

Living by Faith in Turbulent Times

Copyright © 2020 Jonathan Griffiths

Published by: H&E Publishing, Peterborough, Canada
www.hesedandemet.com

All rights reserved. This book or any portion thereof may not be reproduced or used in any manner whatsoever without the express written permission of the publisher except for the use of brief quotations in a book review.

Unless otherwise indicated, all Scripture quotations are from The ESV® Bible (The Holy Bible, English Standard Version®), copyright © 2001 by Crossway, a publishing ministry of Good News Publishers. Used by permission. All rights reserved.

Paperback ISBN: 978-1-989174555
eBook ISBN: 978-1-989174-56-2

First Edition, 2020

For Teddy

Contents

Introduction xi

1. True faith 1

2. Seeing with the Eyes of Faith 19

3. Faith for Fearful Times 37

4. Enduring in Faith 53

Scripture Index 70

Introduction

This book has come into being in the midst of the greatest global crisis since the Second World War and the greatest pandemic since the 1918 Spanish Flu. These are indeed tumultuous days, and they are provoking all of us to consider more carefully the foundations upon which our lives are built. How do we live through such days? What resources do we possess to face them?

For the Christian believer, these days call us to consider how to live as true disciples of Jesus Christ in the midst of a crisis, the like of which we have not seen in our lifetime. Many others who do not yet follow Jesus are asking whether the Christian faith can provide hope in such troubled days.

One of the wonderful characteristics of the Bible is its ability to speak into every situation and provide help for every season of life. Hebrews 11 is one of the most famous and familiar chapters of the Bible, and for good reason. Its gallery of the lives of faith of Old Testament believers lays out a rich tapestry of testimonies that show us today what it looks like to live by faith through the ups-and-downs of life. For me, that tapestry has come to have a new vividness and depth of colour during the coronavirus crisis. I have seen afresh how the lives of faith that it recounts were often lived under intense pressure, as the believers of old navigated uncharted and fearful territory. What holds their stories together is their willingness to trust the unchanging God who proves himself faithful time and time again.

Whether you have walked with this God for many years, whether you are new to the faith, or whether you are trying to find out if this God of the Bible can give you hope in troubled times, I trust that you will be helped and encouraged as we walk through this great gallery of faith together in the pages that follow.

These chapters began life as expositions delivered in the empty building of the Metropolitan Bible Church in Ottawa and broadcast online to a church family (and many watching "guests") who were isolated at home in the depths of the pandemic. In this strange time, it has been a joy to know that the church family has been eager to hear the word of God each week and has been seeking together to walk by faith in tumultuous times.

Bringing these expositions to print has only been possible because of the expert and gracious help of Chance Faulkner and his team at H&E, and I would like to express my thanks to them. This project has rested in a particular way on the patience and loving support of my wife, Gemma, and our three children. I am thankful to them, and for the joyful privilege of walking by faith together with them in our home.

Now faith is the assurance of things hoped for, the conviction of things not seen. For by it the people of old received their commendation. By faith we understand that the universe was created by the word of God, so that what is seen was not made out of things that are visible.

By faith Abel offered to God a more acceptable sacrifice than Cain, through which he was commended as righteous, God commending him by accepting his gifts. And through his faith, though he died, he still speaks. By faith Enoch was taken up so that he should not see death, and he was not found, because God had taken him. Now before he was taken he was commended as having pleased God. And without faith it is impossible to please him, for whoever would draw near to God must believe that he exists and that he rewards those who seek him. By faith Noah, being warned by God concerning events as yet unseen, in reverent fear constructed an ark for the saving of his household. By this he condemned the world and became an heir of the righteousness that comes by faith.

Hebrews 11:1-7

1
TRUE FAITH

As I write, the world is living through some of its most turbulent days in modern history. The days of the coronavirus pandemic are extraordinary days. Perhaps with the exception of the generation who remembers the Second World War, few will have seen such widespread disruption to daily life on a global scale. What the actual outcome of all this will be is yet unknown, but the disruption to normal life, the fear, and the widespread panic are all too real. We are confronted urgently with the question of how to navigate these days as authentic followers of Jesus Christ. What will it look like simply to live as Christian people in such turbulent times?

To begin to answer that question, there can hardly be a more relevant passage of Scripture to help us than Hebrews 11 with its famous and definitive treatment of what it means to live by faith. If there is one thing that must define us in these troubled times, it must be this: *faith*. In a hopeless and panicking world, Christian believers must stand out as those who have faith and live by faith. But as we say that, there is a further question for us to consider: What is faith—*true, authentic faith*—and what does it look like to live out that faith in unsettled times?

The question comes to the fore at the end of Hebrews 10. The writer is wanting to call us to endurance in our walk with

Christ, exhorting us to keep trusting Jesus without giving up: "For you have need of endurance, so that when you have done the will of God you may receive what is promised" (10:35). He then gives as his basis for that call some powerful words that he quotes from the Old Testament book of Habakkuk chapter 2: "For, 'Yet a little while, and the coming one will come and will not delay; but my righteous one shall live by faith, and if he shrinks back, my soul has no pleasure in him'" (10:37-38, citing Habakkuk 2:3-4).

Those who do not have saving faith will face the displeasure of God, even his judgment. But the believing, faith-filled people of God will know his salvation. The righteous people of God are, by definition, a people of faith who will *live by faith*. The writer is confident that he and the people he is addressing are such a people: "But we are not of those who shrink back and are destroyed, but of those who have faith and preserve their souls" (10:39).

Now, the reason why all this is recorded in the Scriptures for us is simple. Like the people first addressed in this letter, we today need to be a people of faith, who persevere in faith, living by faith through times of difficulty and uncertainty.

And so we return to the question: What is faith and what will it look like, in practical terms, to live by faith?

THE DEFINITION OF FAITH

"Now faith is the assurance of things hoped for, the conviction of things unseen." (Hebrews 11:1)

We are a people who appreciate proof, who value evidence, who like to see things with our eyes and feel them with our hands. When it comes to science, we do not take it seriously until we can put it in a test tube and verify it; we know we should not believe it until there have been multiple peer-reviewed studies. When it comes to buying a product, we want to be given a sample, be taken for a test drive, or be shown a thousand verified reviews. We want the opportunity to experience it, and we require the option of returning it if we are unimpressed by it.

That is just how we operate. But, awkward as it may be, there is something about faith that cannot be boiled down in that way. "Faith," Hebrews tells us, "is the assurance of things hoped for, the conviction of things not seen." God by his word makes promises and commitments to us about things that we cannot see or touch or put in a test tube. The word of God gives us hope for the future: hope that God will welcome us into eternal dwellings; hope that we will see our Saviour face-to-face; hope that our life in his immediate presence will be full of joy and free of pain; hope that health and vitality will be our only experience in that age to come, and death and disease will be no more. Faith is having the assurance that God's word is true and that his promises are valid. Faith is having the conviction that the things God tells us about—things we cannot see or feel or account for scientifically—are real and true and substantial.

Faith is no easy thing. It is not something that comes naturally to us. It is something that has always gone against the grain of the skepticism of the sinful nature. The tendency to doubt God's word and his trustworthiness is at the very heart of sin. It goes right back to the Garden of Eden (see Genesis 3). But faith is the polar opposite of sin. Faith has always been the required response of God's own people. The saints of old, Hebrews tells us, were commended for their faith (11:2).

Perhaps the supreme textbook example of a true "faith issue" is the example in verse 3: faith that God made the world. Notice what the writer says: "By faith we understand that the universe was created by the word of God, so that what is seen was not made out of things that are visible" (11:3).

It is fascinating that verse 3 is here at all in this 2000-year-old book. We tend to view skepticism over creation as a modern problem. We tell ourselves that, because we are so very clever and scientifically advanced, we now struggle with this issue in a way that people living in the ancient world never would have. For them, it was just natural to think that God made the world. They did not need to think twice about it. They were primitive, and we are advanced, we tacitly assume.

Well, as it turns out, that is actually not the case. Two thousand years ago, Christian believers recognized that it would require faith to accept God's creation of the world by his word. It has *always* required faith to accept this. None of us was there at the very beginning to watch it happen. God did not record a video of it for us to see. He chose instead to tell us about it, and then to call us to believe.

Now, none of this is to say that belief in God's creation of the world by his word is in any way irrational. The biblical doctrine that God himself made the world and made us is the most rational and coherent explanation for all that we see in this glorious world and all that we are in our human complexity. It actually takes a tremendous leap of faith, along with a dramatic suspension of disbelief, to attribute all this to a random process without any intelligent cause. The very idea stretches credulity beyond any reasonable breaking point.

There are powerful scientific indications and strong rational arguments for believing that God made the world. But, at the end of the day, it requires faith to accept that God made the universe by his word in such a way that what is seen was not made out of things that are visible. And we need to see that God designed it that way. It is not that God simply could not manage to do better. It is not that he found himself unable to provide the kind of proofs that would overcome wilful unbelief. No, God in his wisdom chose for this to be, at the end of the day, a matter of faith.

We humans may long to eradicate the need for faith by putting everything in a test tube. But God delights in our willing and trusting response to his word. Faith is something that pleases God, something that he fundamentally values: "And without faith it is impossible to please him, for whoever would draw near to God must believe that he exists and that he rewards those who seek him" (11:6). Faith, Hebrews insists, is basic to knowing God. We cannot put God in a test tube. We cannot arrive at God by pure reason alone. We have to believe that he exists. We have to respond to his revelation in a posture of faith.

Models of True Faith

Having defined faith, the writer moves to show us some key models of true faith. He begins with three from the book of Genesis for us to observe and learn from as we seek to live lives of faith in our day.

Abel—faith that gives its best

> *"By faith Abel offered to God a more acceptable sacrifice than Cain, through which he was commended as righteous, God commending him by accepting his gifts. And through his faith, though he died, he still speaks."* (Hebrews 11:4)

I wonder if you have ever considered how your faith in God is reflected by what you give to God? It is an interesting thought. What we give to God—in terms of our time and energy and, perhaps most significant in this context, our money and worldly goods—reflects our faith in him, or indeed our lack of faith in him. That is the great lesson that Abel teaches us.

Abel was the second son of Adam. One day, he and his brother Cain both brought gifts to the Lord. On the face of it, both are doing a good and obedient thing. Hebrews tells us, however, that Abel brought by faith a more acceptable sacrifice than his brother and, in so doing, left for us a testimony of faith that still speaks.

To understand the dynamics of this, we should look back to the original story in the Genesis account:

> Now Adam knew Eve his wife, and she conceived and bore Cain, saying, "I have gotten a man with the help of the LORD." And again, she bore his brother Abel. Now Abel was a keeper of sheep, and Cain a worker of the ground. In the course of time Cain brought to the LORD an offering of the fruit of the ground, and Abel also brought of the firstborn of the flock and of their fat portions. And the LORD had regard for Abel and his offering, but for Cain and his

offering he had no regard. So Cain was very angry, and his face fell. (Genesis 4:1–5)

Here are two offerings brought by two brothers. On the face of it, there may seem to be little to choose between them. But, evidently, in the eyes of God, they were markedly different. What was it about Abel's offering that was pleasing to the Lord in the way that Cain's was not? What is it that Abel models for us in terms of *faith* when it comes to his offering?

Well, the detail given here in the Genesis account is sparse without question, but what is given is clearly significant. Cain, for his part, brought "an offering of the fruit of the ground." He was a farmer who grew crops, and he duly brought something from his crop for the Lord. That sounds reasonable enough; it sounds fine to our ears. Next comes Abel and his offering. He was a farmer too; he raised sheep.

Now, before we go further there is something quite wonderful for us to observe and consider. Right here, in Genesis 4, we are given a beautiful little picture of the gospel. Abel could not possibly have known all this in his day, but *we today know* that God would only be satisfied when the perfect Lamb is offered for sin. When John the Baptist announced of Jesus, "Behold the Lamb of God, who takes away the sin of the world" (John 1:29), he announced the arrival of the great sacrifice that would please God and atone for sin. This is a rich gospel hint and pointer within the Genesis story that draws our eyes to Christ. It is a beautiful thing to observe when we set this Genesis event within the broad canvas of the great story of salvation in Christ. But that does not exhaust all that is taking place here in the narrative. There are some simple but profound lessons to learn from Abel and his model of faith.

As we compare Cain and Abel's gifts, we find that while Cain gave *some of the fruit* of his labour, Abel's attitude was of a different kind: he brought an offering of the "firstborn" of the flock and gave of the "fat portions." While Cain gave *something*, Abel gave *the first and the best*. In that action, we learn something profound about the essence of faith. Think about Abel giving the *firstborn*. If you are a farmer raising livestock, the firstborn of your flock is your hope for the future. You do not know if there will be others born. You do not know what else will come. But you know you have your firstborn of the season, the start of a new generation, your hope for feeding your family for the months ahead, and your hope of a future flock to come.

In the ancient world, farmers did not have Manulife or State Farm or Shepherd's Mutual (pick your real or fictional insurance provider!) to fall back on, nor did they have pensions. All they really had was this: they had the firstborn of their flock as security and hope for the future. And Abel, by giving the firstborn to the Lord, was saying to him: "I place my economic security in your hands, and I entrust myself to you. I place my future in your hands, and I wait for your provision. I do not know if there will be other lambs born this season, but the first is for you. I entrust myself to you."

Added to the fact that he gave the firstborn, Abel gave the "fat portions" of the flock to the Lord. He not only gave the first, he also gave the best. He looked out over his flock, and he took the very best of the sheep: the chubby ones, the ones that would make for the best banquets at his table, the ones that would fetch the best price at market. If, in giving the firstborn, he was saying to the Lord, "I believe that you are trustworthy," in giving the best he was saying, "I believe that you are of supreme worth. I cannot see you with my eyes, but by faith I know that you are the God who is worthy of my very best." Genesis tells us that God looked on Abel's offering and had regard for it. God commended Abel as a righteous man, Hebrews tells us. It is not that Abel won his salvation by a great act of giving. No, God saw in Abel's giving concrete evidence of true, saving faith, and it pleased him.

We want to be those who live lives of faith in our uncertain days. We need, therefore, to ask ourselves: Does our material response to God (through our generosity to his people and his work) flow from faith? Does our material response to God give evidence of saving faith within our heart? In days when the world economy is in crisis, and many jobs are looking precarious, and many retirement funds have been impacted, will our handling of our money and possessions flow from faith, or fear?

As an act of faith, as a reflection of our trust in the Lord, will we give the first fruits of our possessions, our finances, our time, our gifts, all the while trusting God for the future? As an act of faith, will we give God our very best—the best of our energy, the best of our abilities, the best of our time, the rich portions of our finances and possessions—even as Abel did? Or will we follow Cain and give him only *something*?

Enoch—the faith that conquers death

"By faith Enoch was taken up so that he should not see death, and he was not found, because God had taken him. Now before he was taken he was commended as having pleased God. And without faith it is impossible to please him, for whoever would draw near to

LIVING BY FAITH

God must believe that he exists and that he rewards those who seek him." (Hebrews 11:5)

As a society we have been forced to confront the ugliness of death in a very immediate way through the coronavirus pandemic. The reality of facing a health crisis we cannot immediately control or combat has shaken our society to the core. It has shaken us because death is a fearful thing. It has shaken us because death shatters all our comfortable illusions of security and stability. Death is a fearful and unavoidable reality of life in a fallen world.

But, for us who know Christ, we know that death has been defeated; we know that there is hope. Enoch is one who teaches us the wonderful power of true faith in defeating death. His brief story is intriguing, but Genesis 5 (where it appears) is a passage we might easily skim over without much attention. It is a genealogy, a list of Adam's descendants down to Noah and his family. On the face of it, this genealogy might not seem all that interesting to us. However, to understand what is going on here and the significance of it, we need to place this chapter in its wider context, within the storyline of Genesis as a whole.

Only four chapters before, God had created a perfect world free of sin and suffering and death. But Adam and Eve rebelled and sin entered the world. God's judgment for sin was death, meaning that, suddenly, this world of abundant life became a place of inescapable death. The genealogy drives home this point with its repetitive drumbeat of gloom. Just notice with me how it goes.

For each generation, we learn that the person lived, had some children, lived some more—and then died. Notice how each paragraph and each generation ends: "Thus all the days that Adam lived were 930 years, and he died...and he died...and he died...and he died...and he died...and he died...and he died." Again and again, the grim drumbeat of death that punctuates life in this fallen world. But then we come to a different kind of man, a different kind of story. We come to a startling break in the pattern:

> When Enoch had lived 65 years, he fathered Methuselah. Enoch walked with God after he fathered Methuselah 300 years and had other sons and daughters. Thus all the days of Enoch were 365 years. Enoch walked with God, and he was not, for God took him. (Genesis 5:21-24)

In all the generations before Enoch, for hundreds of years, there is no mention of the Lord in this genealogy; no mention of walking with him; no mention of anything, really, beyond living and having children, living some more, and eventually dying. As we know the story of Genesis, we know that the people were drifting further from the Lord and the earth was filling with wickedness. And so, in this run of generations where there is no mention of the Lord and only the grim pattern of death upon death, Enoch stands out like a sore thumb. He stands out as a man who does one thing of note, and one thing only: *he walks with God.*

In his eternal being, God is not visible. People do not normally see him or hear his voice in an audible way. Yet, in the largely faithless age represented by Genesis 5, Enoch has the faith to not only believe that God exists, but to live in personal relationship with him, walking with him day-by-day, responding to his word, depending upon him, and seeking to please him. That is the basic insight of the life of Enoch. Hebrews tells us that Enoch was one who pleased God because he had faith.

What then happened to Enoch? In a miracle of grace, God spared him death, and took him to be with himself. And so, in the life of this man of faith, we see the grim drumbeat of death silenced, the harrowing pattern broken. What is the lesson for us? It is simply this: if we would escape the curse and judgment of death and be spared the ultimate outworking of death in hell itself, we must be those who have true *faith* in God as he has made himself known to us in Jesus Christ. We must have faith that believes that he exists, faith that draws near to him, faith that walks with him day-by-day.

The grim drumbeat of death is sounding all around the world today. The Genesis 5 pattern is repeating itself in real time, as it always has since the Fall. In the time of the pandemic, the global media is full of pictures of overflowing mortuaries and mass graves in countries that would have considered themselves well beyond such desperate measures because of their wealth and healthcare resources. Where is hope to be found for escaping this pattern, this drumbeat, this mortal fate? It is in knowing God; it is in walking with God; it is in having faith. In days of widespread fear and panic, Christians are those who know the living God, who walk with him, and who have certain hope of life through him. In days when it seems as though the earth might give way, we are called simply to this: to walk with God in faith.

The image of walking with God is a wonderful picture for us. As a father of young children, there is hardly anything I delight in more than walking alongside one of my children and finding they put their hand in mine, so that we walk together. For a parent, that is a special joy. As followers of Jesus, you and

I may, in faith, place our hand into the hand of God. We listen to his voice through his word, and we go forward in trust. We do that knowing that God will do for us what he does for all who walk with him in faith: he will spare us that final sentence of death and give to us the gift of life beyond the grave.

As we walk like that, steadily and trustingly each day, we show the world that we have a distinctive and crisis-defying trust, hope, security, joy, and peace.

Noah—the faith that condemns the world

"By faith Noah, being warned by God concerning events as yet unseen, in reverent fear constructed an ark for the saving of his household. By this he condemned the world and became an heir of the righteousness that comes by faith." (Hebrews 11:7)

It is always hard to know how seriously to take warnings. The world has been in the business of hearing and responding to warnings a great deal in the time of the pandemic. National leaders, doctors, and individual citizens have all had to evaluate warnings concerning this great health threat, considering carefully what to make of them and what to do with them. As a general rule, those who took the warnings seriously from an early point and took careful precautions have not come to regret that decision.

In a wicked and godless age, the Lord warned one man, Noah, that he was going to act in judgment upon the world. The familiar story is told in Genesis 6. God says that he will bring a flood of judgment upon the earth because of humanity's wickedness. He gives Noah a special warning and calls him to build an ark in preparation for the judgment to come. This Ark would be a great boat designed to save himself and his family, along with the various species of animals in the world. When the sky is blue, and there is not a drop of rain anywhere to be seen, God tells Noah to go and make a boat in his backyard, in preparation for the judgment to come. Noah's response was, in reverent fear, to build that Ark.

You can only imagine what the neighbours must have thought and the gossipy chatter that must have circulated in the local market: "Crazy old Noah building his crazy old boat...spending all his money, taking all his time, obsessively giving himself to that silly project, that fool's errand." However, Noah had heard the word of God. He knew the warning of the judgment to come, he believed God's promise of these events yet unseen, and he duly responded by building the Ark.

Hebrews tells us that, by doing this, "he condemned the world" (11:7). By his behaviour and without anger or malice, he said to those around him that this world was heading for grave danger, even destruction. As Noah's neighbours were giving their time and energy to things of this world, living ungodly lives (and it was an ungodly generation, Genesis 6:5-8 tells us), going about their daily business without regard for the Creator, they did it all in the shadow of Noah's increasingly large boat. They did all this in sight of Noah's faith-driven declaration that judgment was coming.

God tells us in his word today that a day of judgment is coming when he will call his enemies to account and punish the wicked, consigning them to the place of everlasting punishment (see Luke 13:24-28; 2 Peter 3:1-13). We have heard the warning ourselves, and the right response to that is a life of reverent fear. The right response is to live a life of preparation for the judgment to come. It should be the case that the life of the

Christian believer sends that message of warning to the world. It should be that the world looks on at the believer's life and is confused and perplexed: "Why is he doing that? Why is she giving her time to that? Why is he refraining from doing what we are doing? Why is his life so distinctive? Why are her words, her actions, her values, and her priorities so unlike anyone else's?" If we take the warnings of judgment seriously in our day, if we live the life of faith, our very lives will act as a giant warning sign to the world that there is something terrible coming for which the world needs to be ready. In that sense we will speak of the world's condemnation, not for the sake of condemnation, but for the sake of salvation. If we live distinctively, as a people who fear God and await his judgment of the world, then, by God's grace, others may look on, take notice, and be willing to hear of the salvation that we ourselves have received.

The world has always needed this, of course. But we are in a special season of opportunity for gospel witness. The coronavirus pandemic has shaken our world to its very core, and the dislocation of this crisis will last for years to come, casting its shadow well into the future. We who know the Lord have an opportunity to bear witness to the Lord Jesus and his great salvation by living the life of faith in these unsettled days. Our call, opportunity, and responsibility in these days is simple: it is to live by faith. It is to live by the faith that gives God the very best, the faith that defeats death, and the faith that condemns the world.

May God strengthen and encourage us to be people of true faith—authentic Christian faith—who live by that faith in the days to come, whatever they may bring.

By faith Abraham obeyed when he was called to go out to a place that he was to receive as an inheritance. And he went out, not knowing where he was going. By faith he went to live in the land of promise, as in a foreign land, living in tents with Isaac and Jacob, heirs with him of the same promise. For he was looking forward to the city that has foundations, whose designer and builder is God. By faith Sarah herself received power to conceive, even when she was past the age, since she considered him faithful who had promised. Therefore from one man, and him as good as dead, were born descendants as many as the stars of heaven and as many as the innumerable grains of sand by the seashore.

These all died in faith, not having received the things promised, but having seen them and greeted them from afar, and having acknowledged that they were strangers and exiles on the earth. For people who speak thus make it clear that they are seeking a homeland. If they had been thinking of that land from which they had gone out, they would have had opportunity to return. But as it is, they desire a better country, that is, a heavenly one. Therefore God is not ashamed to be called their God, for he has prepared for them a city.

By faith Abraham, when he was tested, offered up Isaac, and he who had received the promises was in the act of offering up his only son, of whom it was said, "Through Isaac shall your offspring be named." He considered that God was able even to raise him from the dead, from which, figuratively speaking, he did receive him back. By faith Isaac invoked future blessings on Jacob and Esau. By faith Jacob, when dying, blessed each of the sons of Joseph, bowing in worship over the head of his staff. By faith Joseph, at the end of his life, made mention of the exodus of the Israelites and gave direction concerning his bones.

Hebrews 11:8–22

2

SEEING WITH THE EYES OF FAITH

In the midst of the coronavirus pandemic, we came to see that all our plans for the foreseeable future needed to be put on hold, torn up, cancelled, or revised. We thought we knew certain things about today or tomorrow, or next week or next month, but it turned out that we did not know these things after all. We had dreams and hopes for what we intended to do; we had plans laid out for the future. But it turned out that our confidence in our own agenda was entirely misplaced. As the crisis struck and stay-at-home and shelter-in-place orders were issued around the globe, the world collectively had to tear up its plans. Perhaps you remember where you were meant to be and what you were meant to be doing when the crisis struck. Perhaps you had plans for a vacation, plans to visit family, plans to start a new job, plans to get married, or plans to move to a new home. It never occurred to most of us that our plans would not be fulfilled.

All this teaches us a lesson that the Bible would have taught us, if we paid attention: worldly plans and projections for the future are simply not reliable or trustworthy. We cannot see into the future to observe the coming hours, let alone the coming days or weeks. We do not have that kind of sight (see James 4:13-17). However, Hebrews wants to show us that faith gives us another kind of sight—another kind of *insight* into the days to come. In the previous chapter we considered Hebrews' definition of faith, that is, "the assurance of things hoped for, the conviction of things not seen" (Hebrews 11:1). Because God has told us much about what is to come and has made commitments about the future in his word, if we look into that future with the eyes of faith, we can place our hope in what he has said.

The original readers of Hebrews needed help to see with the eyes of faith. We know that these believers had previously faced deep trials in their Christian life. At the end of chapter 10 (in verses 32-34), the writer reminds them of some gruelling experiences that they had faced in days gone by: suffering, exposure to reproach and affliction, and the loss of property and possessions. That was their former experience, and it is quite clear that now, at the time of this letter, they are facing renewed trials.

Throughout Hebrews, the writer pleads with these believers not to give up on following Christ. As we survey the whole book, we get a fairly clear sense of the kind of thing that is probably happening. Hebrews is grounded in deep and sustained engagement with the Old Testament and with the rites and institutions of Judaism, and the overall shape of its argument, indicates that these believers are from a Jewish background. From what we see in the writer's argument and appeal, it seems quite clear that they are facing pressure to return to the familiar and tangible religious rites of Judaism (at the synagogue or the temple). You can just imagine the kinds of things that their friends and family might be feeling and might be saying to them: "Look, we have promises in God's Law that if we come to the Levitical priests at the temple and offer the required animal sacrifices, all will be well with us. We will be spiritually safe. But now you have abandoned all that concrete, reliable, and God-ordained religion, and you are entrusting yourself to an invisible priest in heaven and to an unseen future hope. This is dangerous; it is reckless. Come back, please, to where there is spiritual safety at the synagogue and the temple."

Added to all that religious pressure, there was a wider social pressure. Judaism was an officially tolerated religion in the Roman Empire. There was at least some safety in being part of that community. However, there was no such official tolerance for being a Christian at this time. That was much more risky. The Romans had only fairly recently crucified the leader of that new "sect," and persecution was a familiar part of the early Christian experience. What these believers needed to learn was simply this: to see with the eyes of faith. They needed to look into the future through the lenses of the promises of God, through the spectacles of the word of God, trusting that God's promises are true and real and substantial.

In our age and in our present circumstances, in order to live through the days of change and uncertainty that we now face, you and I need the very same thing. To help and encourage us in this, Hebrews takes us again to some Old Testament models of faith and shows us from their witness and their experience what it means to *see with the eyes of faith.*

Living by Faith

Seeking God's Homeland

"By faith Abraham obeyed when he was called to go out to a place that he was to receive as an inheritance. And he went out, not knowing where he was going." (Hebrews 11:8)

You may remember the story. God came to Abraham (or, *Abram*, as he was then), tapped him on the shoulder, and said, "Go from your country and your kindred and your father's house to the land that I will show you" (Genesis 12:1). God promised to bless Abraham as he went, and to make him a blessing to the world. Abraham, for his part, responded in faith: "So Abram went, as the LORD had told him" (Genesis 12:4). God called Abraham to leave his home, his wider family, all that he has known, and go to a place of which he knew nothing beyond the fact that God promised to give it to him. And at the call of God, Abraham and his wife Sarah got up and went. They did not have much information or detail, but they trusted God enough to pack their things, leave their home behind, and depart.

These days, when we plan to travel, we turn to TripAdvisor or Expedia and we do our research. We look at the pictures of our destination. We get images of the restaurants and the food, of the pool at the hotel, of the attractions and amusements. Before we have left our living room at home, we have a pretty clear picture of where we are going. Abraham and Sarah had none of that. They were going to "the land that I will show you." That is all they had to go on. But for them, it was enough, and they went.

Interestingly, though, their reason for going was not that they thought this land of promise would be great. No, their reason for going was actually that they were looking beyond their next stop on the journey to something far greater, something they could only see with the eyes of faith:

> By faith he went to live in the land of promise, as in a foreign land, living in tents with Isaac and Jacob, heirs with him of the same promise. For he was looking forward to the city that has foundations, whose designer and builder is God. (Hebrews 11:9-10)

God gave Abraham the faith to believe that, beyond their immediate destination in this physical land, there was an eternal homeland prepared for them. Beyond any city that might be built in Canaan, the Lord had prepared a greater city, Zion above. By giving him faith that he would not only provide a temporal home but an eternal home, God set Abraham free of concern for his former home. As the Lord gave Abraham the eyes of faith to see his eternal home, he loosened his grip on his earthly home. Such a faith-fuelled outlook is fundamental to authentic faith. This is at the very core of what it means to have faith in God, his promises, and his provision.

The writer looks back at the heroes of faith he has mentioned thus far (Abel, Enoch, Noah, Abraham, Sarah) and says this about them:

> These all died in faith, not having received the things promised, but having seen them and greeted them from afar, and having acknowledged that they were strangers and exiles on earth. For people who speak thus make it clear that they are seeking a homeland.

> If they had been thinking of that land from which they had gone out, they would have had opportunity to return. But as it is, they desire a better country, that is, a heavenly one. Therefore God is not ashamed to be called their God, for he has prepared for them a city. (Hebrews 11:13–16)

People of faith have the eyes of their hearts set on things they do not receive in full in this life. The promises of God point us beyond this life to the life to come. While we have a taste and an experience of God's presence and his salvation now, we enter into the full reality in the life to come. The people of faith of ages past died in faith, greeting these things from afar.

Just recently I had the opportunity to visit a member of our church family at the hospital not long before she went to be with the Lord. She was very weak and very frail, but in the years I had known her, I had never seen her look quite so peaceful. Although ravaged by disease, she was almost radiant with joy. We spoke about the Lord and her experience of knowing and serving him from her youth. We talked about heaven and the prospect of being in his presence and being reunited there as his people. She was there dying in a hospital bed, having been struck down by aggressive cancer, and yet her eyes were fixed on the city to come, Jerusalem above. The eyes of her heart were fixed on heaven. And I was reminded that people who think like that and talk like that and live like that make it clear that they are seeking their homeland.

Some years ago I was involved in a ministry to young people. Many of the kids and teenagers we reached through this ministry were from quite a privileged background, and I always remember how some of the leaders within the ministry used to pray that the Lord in his kindness might "spoil the world" for these kids. "Lord, please spoil the world for them." That was a very striking prayer to pray. But the spiritual insight behind it was profound: these kids had it so good in worldly terms, the best thing that could happen for them would be to fall out of love with this world. The best thing for them would be if the Lord, in his kindness, might remove the sheen from this present world and spoil its perfection in their eyes in some way.

The saints of old (Abraham, Sarah, and others) could have turned back to the place from which they came. Abraham could have got cold feet and gone back home. But he, like the others, desired "a better country, a heavenly one" (11:16). One of the ways the Lord has used the great pandemic already is to spoil the world for us in some ways. At the start of the crisis, many had wonderful vacation plans for spring break, but they went quickly down the drain. Many had wonderful stock portfolios, and those too were severely impacted. Many had growing businesses and notable worldly success, yet many businesses and enterprises have been terribly affected. None of these losses is pleasant. None of these circumstances is good in itself. Some are absolutely dreadful. As we have felt those material effects of this crisis, one good outcome of all the carnage may be this: just maybe we will fall out of love with this present world, and maybe we will learn to set the eyes of our heart on the homeland above that God has prepared for us.

I have been thinking often of late of John Newton's great hymn about Zion above, "Glorious Things of Thee Are Spoken." It so resonates with the heart of Abraham, and I believe it is a hymn for our age:

> *Glorious things of thee are spoken,*
>   *Zion, city of our God;*
> *he, whose word cannot be broken,*
>   *formed thee for his own abode:*
> *on the Rock of ages founded,*
>   *what can shake thy sure repose?*
> *With salvation's walls surrounded,*
>   *thou may'st smile on all thy foes.*
>
> *Saviour, if of Zion's city*
>   *I through grace, a member am,*
> *let the world deride or pity,*
>   *I will glory in Thy name:*
> *fading is the worldling's pleasure,*
>   *all his boasted pomp and show;*
> *solid joys and lasting treasure*
>   *none but Zion's children know.*

Those who see with the eyes of faith seek God's homeland.

Trusting God's Life-Giving Power

The great barrier to the greatest promises of God is the barrier of physical frailty and death. God promised Abraham and Sarah many descendants, but they were past age. God promises all his people an eternal future in his heavenly home, but the looming reality of death would seem to deny us the very life for which we long. Death is, of course, humanity's main problem. I hardly need to tell you that. If we had somehow forgotten that reality or blocked it out, we have now been reminded, each one of us, by the great pandemic. Death lurks around the corner of our experience and at the gates of our community all the time.

That is always true, pandemic or none. It is so striking how powerless we are in the face of death. Our healthcare is so advanced and our medical resources so wonderful in many countries. We tend to imagine that no illness or disease is beyond the healing reach of modern medicine. And yet, the most advanced nations in the world, the most capable scientists, and the most competent physicians have been able to offer nothing to stem the tide of this pandemic in its early months. Hundreds of thousands have died, and the world's best resources have offered little help at all. Early in the crisis, harrowing news reports showed footage from inside a very fine and modern hospital in Lombardy, Italy (a nation with good healthcare by global standards), but the scenes were of helplessness in the face of death. Modern medicine, even the best of it, has been no match for the pandemic. Death is not defeatable by human beings. That is the bottom line. We are learning that grim truth afresh.

However, fundamental to biblical faith is the belief that God's power is greater than physical frailty, even death itself. Consider Sarah. God promises that she and Abraham will be parents to a great nation that will bring blessing to the earth. It is a stunning promise. However, in physical and human terms, it actually becomes an impossible promise. No child arrives, and Abraham and Sarah are well beyond age. And so, for them to believe that God could keep this promise ultimately took great faith:

> By faith Sarah herself received power to conceive, even when she was past the age, since she considered him faithful who had promised. Therefore from one man, and him as good as dead, were born descendants as many as the stars of heaven and as many as

the innumerable grains of sand on the seashore. (Hebrews 11:11)

If you know the story, you will know that Abraham and Sarah had their own wobbles on this. They tried to take matters into their own hands when it looked like God was not coming through (Genesis 16). But ultimately God taught them to trust him and to wait on him. All his promises for Abraham and the nation rested on Abraham and Sarah being given a son. In what has to be called a miracle, God gave this old couple, well beyond age, the promised son. He gave them Isaac, who would be the conduit to the fulfilment of all God's promises (Genesis 21). He would bring into existence the nation. As we read our Bibles onward, we learn that Jesus himself traced his ancestry through this nation, through this son of Abraham (see Matthew 1:2). Our salvation in Christ rested upon God overcoming physical frailty and decline to bring life from bodies that were on their way to the grave.

But in case Abraham and Sarah failed to learn the lesson of God's life-giving power, and in case you and I did not learn it from their story, God reinforced it in a dramatic way. Having given Isaac to Abraham and Sarah, fulfilling the promise by this great miracle, God did something very surprising indeed. A few chapters later, he called upon Abraham to take Isaac up a mountain and sacrifice him on an altar (Genesis 22). It was a tremendous test of faith and obedience for Abraham. Here was his only son, who came by way of a divine miracle and who was the only means by which the promises could be fulfilled, and now the call was to offer him up and take his life.

If you know the story, you will remember what happens next. Abraham takes his boy up the hill, builds an altar, places

SEEING WITH THE EYES OF FAITH

him on it, raises the blade, is ready to kill him in obedience to God's instruction, and at that final moment he hears a message from God himself, instructing him not to kill the boy. A ram then appears, and Abraham is to offer the ram instead. The Lord himself has provided a substitute. Abraham had learned to trust God's life-giving power, and so, when tested, he trusted God's voice and did what God said. He did that, even though he knew that the promises of God were to be fulfilled through Isaac. By faith, "He considered that God was able even to raise him from the dead, from which, figuratively speaking, he did receive him back" (11:19). Ultimately, to go up that mountain and build that altar and lay his son upon it and raise that blade, he had to consider that God's power over death was limitless. Not only could God enable ancient bodies to conceive, reckoned Abraham, he could even restore life to a slaughtered son.

In the kindness of God, this was a serious test for Abraham, *but not more than a test*. At the same time, we know that the test of Abraham pointed forward to the very reality that God the Father would embrace in full measure centuries later. On a mount outside Jerusalem—some suggest that it may even be the same mount upon which Abraham built that altar—the very Son of God would be pierced and stricken and slaughtered. The blade would not be stopped; this would be no mere test. The Son of God would die for the sin of others, even for your sin and mine.

But even there—*especially there, ultimately there*—what Abraham reckoned by faith was shown to be true. God has resurrection power. For his Son, the grave was not the end. If the promises of God rested in any way on Abraham's son, they rested a thousand times more on God's own Son. Had Jesus died and not risen, all God's promises would be void and all hope of his people disappointed. But God is the God of life-giving power. God is the God who defeats the grave. And so, on the third day, Jesus rose. On the third day, the promises of God were validated and confirmed and fulfilled.

Christian faith, at its core, is faith in God's life-giving power. It is faith in God's power over the grave. And it is precisely that faith—*simple and authentic Christian faith*—that we need today. Death has become our world's grim fixation through the recent pandemic. It has become something that our communities have had to confront in new ways and in greater measure of late. For such a time, we need to be those who cling to the belief and hold to the hope that our God is the God of life-giving power. He is the God who gives life beyond the grave to those who believe his promises and trust in his Son.

Do you have that kind of confidence and that kind of faith? Perhaps recent events have caused you to look for hope in a way that you have never felt the need to look for it before. Perhaps you are looking for life beyond the grave. The God of the Bible is the God who gives life to the dead. He promises life to those who come to him and trust in him. He proved his life-giving power by raising Jesus from the grave, and he promises to use that same life-giving power to raise us to new life, if we will entrust ourselves to him (see Ephesians 1:18–20). He promises to give this life to all who will turn from rebellion against him and find forgiveness through his Son. Have you done that? And if not, would you do it, even today?

Seeing with the Eyes of Faith

Confidence in God's Purposes and Plans

"By faith Jacob, when dying, blessed each of the sons of Joseph, bowing in worship over the head of his staff. By faith Joseph, at the end of his life, made mention of the exodus of the Israelites and gave directions concerning his bones." (Hebrews 11:21)

I do not know what you would want to be remembered for after you die. Most of us would probably want to be remembered for some of the key activities of our life, for the relationships we were engaged in, and for the projects we completed over the years. It is interesting that, for these two heroes of faith, Hebrews focuses on what they did—or, more precisely, *what they said*—at the time of their death.

Jacob was the great patriarch of the twelve tribes of Israel. We are told that when he died, he bowed in worship over the head of his staff and blessed two of his grandsons, the two sons of Joseph. He asked the Lord to "bless the boys; and in them let my name be carried on, and the name of my fathers Abraham and Isaac; and let them grow into a multitude in the midst of the earth" (Genesis 48:16). Jacob's own life was at an end. He knew that. He and his family were living in the land of Egypt, not in their own promised land. He knew that too. But he also knew that God had made promises to his ancestor Abraham; promises to his family; promises for the future. He knew that God had plans, and he saw with the eyes of faith that those plans were not finished, and would not fail. And so his final act was to gather to him the future of his family, first his grandsons, and after that all his sons, to bless them, calling upon the Lord to fulfil his plans and purposes through the generations to come.

Almost immediately in the Genesis account we learn next of the death of Joseph, one of Jacob's sons. Joseph's words from his deathbed are similarly significant:

> And Joseph said to his brothers, "I am about to die, but God will visit you and bring you up out of this land to the land that he swore to Abraham, to Isaac, and to Jacob." Then Joseph made the sons of Israel swear, saying, "God will surely visit you, and you shall carry up my bones from here." (Genesis 50:24-25)

Joseph was dying in Egypt, but he knew that Egypt was not the final destination of the people of God. He remembered that God had sworn to bring his people into the land of promise. Because he knew God's plans could not fail, his final request was for his bones to be taken out of Egypt and placed in the land of promise. With his final breath, he expressed confidence in God's faithfulness. Both these men of faith ended their lives with a declaration that God's promises would stand and his plans would be fulfilled. Yes, they were in the wrong land. Yes, they themselves were dying and could contribute nothing more to the fulfillment of God's purposes. But they saw into the future with the eyes of faith.

The Bible tells us that God's plan and purpose is to build his church in such a way that the gates of hell itself will not prevail against it (Matthew 16:17-19). God's purpose is to bring the gospel to the ends of the earth. God's purpose is to save a people for himself, a people who will love him, serve him, and grow in holiness while awaiting his return. And there are days when we wonder if God's plan will work and his purpose prevail. There have been key times in church history when, in human terms, the work of the gospel should have been brought to a complete halt. The history of the church in China in the mid-twentieth century is a case in point. Foreign missionaries were expelled from the country after the events of 1949, with churches shut down or forced to go underground. And for decades the Western Church imagined that all the years invested in missions in China had now come to nothing. It looked as though the plans and purposes of God had been defeated. Then, decades later, China opened up to the wider world, and the global church discovered, to its surprise, that church growth had exploded during those silent decades. There had been a quiet revival. The blood of the martyrs had been the seed of the church, and the gates of hell had not prevailed.

On a normal day in any given country in the West, the cultural headwinds blow strongly against the church of Jesus Christ. Wider society is so out of sync with the word of God, so resistant to the message of his grace. And, as Christians, we may wonder: Can God's plans be fulfilled; will his purposes stand? The question is often made more urgent in a time of crisis. One of the first responses to the pandemic was for governments around the world to place limitations on large gatherings of people. Churches had to stop meeting. Bible study groups, youth groups, Sunday schools, and evangelistic discussion groups all had to stop getting together. So we ask the question: Will this now stop the work of the gospel? Will this thwart the purposes of God for the church and the world?

Time will tell, of course, what will be the fruit of all this. However, the earliest indications are that the coronavirus crisis has led to an immensely fruitful period of ministry. God's people have been hungry for God's word. Brothers and sisters in

Christ have been longing for fellowship and have been keen to care for one another. It seems as though those on the margins and sidelines have gained a new spiritual appetite. By God's grace, through technology, we are able to speak and receive the word of God remotely. Churches in many different locations report digital audiences for the preaching of God's word that have swelled by thousands of people. The basic point is this: the word of God will not be chained (2 Timothy 2:9). God's plans for the church and for the kingdom will not be slowed down. The Lord Jesus Christ will return on the day of the Father's eternal choice, just as planned. Yes, the people of God were in Egypt not Canaan. Yes, Jacob died in the wrong place. But he blessed his grandsons in faith, knowing that God's purpose would stand for the future. Yes, Joseph died in a foreign land, but he was so sure that the Exodus would happen, that he gave instructions for his lifeless bones to be carried to the land of promise.

Yes, the work of the gospel faces huge obstacles in our day, just as it always has. It will surely face new obstacles in the years to come. But we can trust that the gates of hell will not prevail against God's church as he builds it. And so, by the grace of God, guided by the word of God, we look into the future—trustingly, joyfully, confidently—with the eyes of faith.

By faith Moses, when he was born, was hidden for three months by his parents, because they saw that the child was beautiful, and they were not afraid of the king's edict. By faith Moses, when he was grown up, refused to be called the son of Pharaoh's daughter, choosing rather to be mistreated with the people of God than to enjoy the fleeting pleasures of sin. He considered the reproach of Christ greater wealth than the treasures of Egypt, for he was looking to the reward. By faith he left Egypt, not being afraid of the anger of the king, for he endured as seeing him who is invisible. By faith he kept the Passover and sprinkled the blood, so that the Destroyer of the firstborn might not touch them.

By faith the people crossed the Red Sea as on dry land, but the Egyptians when they attempted to do the same, were drowned. By faith the walls of Jericho fell down after they had been encircled for seven days. By faith Rahab the prostitute did not perish with those who were disobedient, because she had given a friendly welcome to the spies.

And what more shall I say? For time would fail me to tell of Gideon, Barak, Samson, Jephthah, of David and Samuel and the prophets—who through faith conquered kingdoms, enforced justice, obtained promises, stopped the mouths of lions, quenched the power of fire, escaped the edge of the sword, were made strong out of weakness, became mighty in war, put foreign armies to flight. Women received back their dead by resurrection. Some were tortured, refusing to accept release, so that they might rise again to a better life. Others suffered mocking and flogging, and even chains and imprisonment. They were stoned, they were sawn in two, they were killed with the sword. They went about in skins of sheep and goats, destitute, afflicted, mistreated— of whom the world was not worthy—wandering about in deserts and mountains, and in dens and caves of the earth.

And these, though commended through their faith, did not receive what was promised, since God had provided something better for us, that apart from us they should not be made perfect.

Hebrews 11:23–40

3

FAITH FOR FEARFUL TIMES

If there is one emotion that has characterized the time of the coronavirus pandemic, one feeling shared by millions around the world, it is simply this: *fear*. The crisis has caused many among us to be fearful for our world, for our communities, for our loved ones, and for ourselves. There is no doubt; the pandemic has made for a fearful time. It may be that you share something of that sense of fear. Perhaps you are looking for security and hope. You have been prompted by recent events to consider spiritual realities in a new way, with a new depth, and perhaps a new urgency. What are we to do with this fear? How are we to manage our fear?

For us who know and love Jesus Christ, we need to consider carefully how we are to live by faith during fearful times. In situations where it might seem entirely rational to be afraid, what will it look like to live distinctively as the people of God?

The writer of Hebrews wrote chapter 11 to help us understand what it is to live by faith in any season of life. That has been his focus from the outset of this famous chapter. He set out this concern and this agenda at the end of the previous chapter, quoting words from the Old Testament book of Habakkuk: "Yet a little while and the coming one will come and not delay; but my righteous one shall live by faith, and if he shrinks back, my soul has no pleasure in him" (10:37-38, quoting Habakkuk 2:3-4). The writer wants us to be those who live by faith, and now in this final section of chapter 11, he sets out to show us what it means to live by faith in the particular context of fearful times. He invites us to walk with him through stories of Old Testament believers who lived through fearful times and fearful experiences, but who did so in steadfast faith. Through these stories, he wants us to take hold of a very grand lesson. He wants us to see that God has used fearful circumstances again and again in the lives of his people. He wants us to see that these circumstances have not derailed God's plans for salvation and for his church, but have actually been part of the very fabric of his purposes and his plans. He wants us to see and believe that *God works salvation as his people walk by faith through fearful times.*

MOSES' PARENTS

"By faith Moses, when he was born, was hidden for three months by his parents, because they saw that the child was beautiful, and they were not afraid of the king's edict." (Hebrews 11:23)

At the time of Moses' birth, the people of Israel were living in slavery in Egypt. They had gone to Egypt originally in a time of famine because Joseph, one of their own, was in leadership and welcomed them and cared for them. But, as the opening of the book of Exodus tells us, there arose another king in Egypt who did not know Joseph and did not have regard for his family, the people of Israel. As the Israelites grew in number, Pharaoh became frightened of their potential to threaten him, and so an evil plan was hatched to control their population by killing all the baby boys. It was a heinous, genocidal plot. These were dark and frightening days for the people of God.

At the same time, it is quite wonderful to read the story as it unfolds in the book of Exodus. Once the awful news of Pharaoh's plan is shared in Exodus 1, chapter 2 opens with a simple scene from everyday life and a hopeful indication that life will continue despite the darkness: "Now a man from the house of Levi went and took as his wife a Levite woman" (Exodus 2:1). A young couple have fallen in love. Despite being slaves in a foreign land and despite the storm clouds gathering over them, life continues, and they marry. Then comes news of a baby: "The woman conceived and bore a son, and when she saw that he was a fine child, she hid him three months" (Exodus 2:2). Moses' mother sees that this is a fine child. Being a Hebrew, she would know that this fine and beautiful child was a gift of God, made in his image. She would know that the murder of this child would be a terrible crime, an awful sin against God himself. And so, risking her own life (and no doubt acting in tandem with her husband), she hides the child.

The ensuing narrative is famous and familiar. When baby Moses grows too big to be hidden anymore in the home, his mother makes a basket for him and places this basket in the river, among the reeds at the riverbank. The word that the book of Exodus uses to describe this little floating "basket" is an unusual word, the same word used in Genesis 6 to speak of Noah's Ark. This is a little vessel of salvation, a little boat through which God will bring about his saving plan. Sure enough, that is just what God does: Pharaoh's daughter goes down to the river to bathe, sees the basket and the baby, and decides that she will take pity on him. Moses' sister is near the riverbank observing, and now appears to volunteer to find a nurse for the baby. She goes and calls Moses' own mother, who now will be paid by the daughter of the murderous king to care for her own baby. In due time, Pharaoh's daughter takes Moses home as her own son.

The child who would have been destroyed by Pharaoh's decree is now welcomed into Pharaoh's household as a son, even a prince. This child would become God's agent of salvation for Israel, the means by which his saving purposes are achieved. This amazing story was all of God's extraordinary design, but at the same time happened through the faith of Moses' parents. Notice again what Hebrews says: "By faith Moses, when he was born, was hidden for three months by his parents, because they saw that the child was beautiful, and they were not afraid of the king's edict" (Hebrews 11:23). This young couple had a basic choice to make. Would they fear the king and give up their son to his cruel decree, or would they trust God for their protection, doing everything in their power to safeguard this God-given gift, this beautiful child entrusted to them? In a fearful time, in the face of the genocidal anger and hatred of a powerful king, they decided to act in faith. God worked through that faith to achieve his saving purposes, not just for a baby, but for a nation, and (as we shall see) for you and for me as well.

MOSES

"By faith Moses, when he was grown up, refused to be called the son of Pharaoh's daughter, choosing rather to be mistreated with the people of God than to enjoy the fleeting pleasures of sin."
(Hebrews 11:24-25)

After he grows up, Moses sees an Egyptian beating a Hebrew (remember that his people are slaves in the land). For Moses, this moment becomes a moment of decision. Will he turn a princely blind eye, pretend he saw nothing, and return to the palace for lunch like a good Egyptian prince? Will he give the Egyptian abuser a conspiratorial wink and a fraternal slap on the back on his way? Or will he stand up to him? Will he cast in his lot with the people of God and defend this victim of abuse, staying the hand of the oppressor? Moses famously chooses the latter, killing the abuser in defense of the defenseless. And in making that choice in that crucial moment of decision, he gives up his royal privilege and makes himself an outcast and a fugitive. He is forced to flee Egypt and leave behind his life of comfort.

Hebrews 11:26 is one of those verses we trip over a little because it surprises us and we don't quite know what to make of it at first. The writer tells us that Moses "considered the reproach of Christ greater wealth than the treasures of Egypt, for he was looking to the reward." In what sense was Moses considering the reproach of Christ *at all* in his day, centuries before Jesus was born in Bethlehem? That's a good question, and probing it just a little actually takes us deep into the fabric of the interconnections of the Bible and of the New Testament's reading of the Old.

In choosing to cast in his lot with his nation of birth, God's chosen people, Moses was saying essentially this: "Yes, the treasures of Egypt are mine now. The pleasures of life in this wicked society are open to me. But I see greater treasure attached to membership of the people of God because they are heirs of the very precious promises of God. God has promised to save us, to bring us into our own land, and to make us a great blessing to the nations." That was the choice he made, but to choose the people of God and the riches of the future promises of God meant choosing for a time to embrace reproach. The people of Israel were slaves, abused, mistreated, and scorned by the world.

When God the Son came to earth as a man, the Bible tells us that he came to be the true Israelite, the faithful and promised son of Abraham who would sum up the hopes of the nation. He came to be the Son of David, the promised Messiah who would deliver the people of God from all that enslaved them. He came to be the representative of Israel, the Saviour of Israel, the Messiah of Israel. And so, when Moses chose to bear the reproach of Israel in his day, Hebrews tells us that he was ultimately choosing the reproach of Christ, who would himself be scorned and abused, even murdered by his oppressors, but who would emerge from the grave gloriously victorious. In choosing to bear the reproach of Israel—with its burdens and needs, but also its divine promises—Moses was choosing to bear the reproach that would be taken up by Christ and fulfilled in Christ. He did not know how God would achieve that salvation, to be sure. He did not have the details of a birth in Bethlehem to come. But he looked forward to the deliverance that would arrive ultimately, through Christ, in accordance with the promises of God. Moses was content to bear that reproach in place of the treasures of Egypt, because he was looking forward to the reward, the fulfilment and enjoyment of the very salvation of God.

That was the choice that Moses made, and so he stepped out in faith and not in fear: "By faith he left Egypt, not being afraid of the anger of the king, for he endured as seeing him who is invisible" (11:27). Whether the writer is talking here about Moses' first departure from Egypt after he killed the abusive Egyptian, or his second departure when he led the whole nation out in the Exodus, is not totally certain. Either way, the bigger point is simple enough: had Moses feared Pharaoh more than God, he would have stayed in Egypt, both on the first occasion and the second. Although this powerful king was thoroughly visible and his anger all too palpable, for Moses, the invisible Sovereign above was of far greater importance. Pleasing him mattered more. Because he was serving the Lord above, Moses endured in his pilgrimage away from security in Egypt, away from the palace, away from those earthly comforts. In doing so, he trusted the Lord's promised protection, keeping the Passover that God ordained for him and the people he led: "By faith he kept the Passover and sprinkled the blood, so that the Destroyer of the firstborn might not touch them" (11:28).

God called Moses not only to walk through dangerous and fearful times but to lead the whole nation through them. Moses was called upon to be God's representative before the greatest superpower and the greatest ruler on earth, ultimately speaking words of judgement upon them. He led Israel through the ten plagues of judgment that God sent upon the land in which they lived. In all this, Moses was called to trust, to wait, and to endure in faith. Of the ten plagues, the greatest and most terrifying was the plague of the death of the firstborn son of each household in the land. God told Moses how to instruct the people to escape the plague. They were to take a lamb without blemish and kill the lamb, putting its blood on the doorposts of the house. The angel of death would then pass over that house and spare its firstborn son. The people were to trust God's promise, both of this coming judgment and of his provision for protection. Moses led the people by faith, through the plague and into salvation.

The Passover was, of course, a great picture that pointed forward to the salvation of Christ, reinforcing the point of verse 26 that all this anticipated Christ. It pointed forward to the clear call of the gospel to take seriously God's warning of a judgment to come, and trust entirely in his provision of salvation in Christ. Yes, a judgment is coming, a day of reckoning when God will call the world to account for rebelling against him. But there is a way of protection, a way of safety. Take cover in the blood of Jesus Christ, the blemish-free Lamb of God who died that you might live.

By faith, Moses kept the Passover (and led the people to keep the Passover) so that Israel was spared. It is interesting to reflect upon the fact that God chose to allow Moses and his family to go through such fearful times. In his sovereignty, he could have preserved Moses' parents and their generation from the horror of Pharaoh's decree. He could have prevented this chosen leader and saviour of Israel from needing to be put into a basket in a crocodile-infested river in the hope of sparing his life in infancy. He could have prevented that ugly scene where Moses saw the Hebrew being beaten. He could have spared Moses the necessity of fleeing for his life. He could have done something other than send the destroying angel to bring judgment upon the land. God's saving purposes could have been achieved another way. But in his sovereignty and wisdom, God called Moses and his family to walk through all this, to endure these truly fearful times, and to do so by faith. To our surprise, it was as they walked in faith through all this—*it was by means of all this*—that God chose to work out his saving purposes and plans.

Of course, the experience of Moses was but a pale foreshadowing of what Jesus endured for us. Jesus faced the anger of the Romans, the hatred of the religious establishment, unjust trials, mocking, beatings, abandonment, and ultimately, crucifixion. He walked through all that with his eyes fixed on his future and joyful hope, as Hebrews 12 goes on to tell us. And the simple reason that Hebrews reminds us of all this is so that we will walk by faith in our day. The writer wants us to run with endurance the race set out before us (12:1).

The Exodus Generation

"By faith the people crossed the Red Sea as on dry land, but the Egyptians, when they attempted to do the same, were drowned."
(Hebrews 11:29)

One of our favourite walks near our home in Canada's capital region is a walk around a pretty lake called Pink Lake in Gatineau Park. The government commission that manages the park has built a great trail (complete with paths and boardwalks and handrails and viewing platforms) to take you all the way around the lake in safety and comfort while enjoying its beauty. In the absence of a boat, the best way to tackle any large body of water is, of course, to go around it, rather than through it (at least under normal circumstances!).

God could have called the Israelites to travel another way than he did. He could have protected them from the pursuing Egyptian army by some other means. But what he chose to do was this: he chose to send them through the middle of the Sea as he held back the water. It was the most awe-inspiring and potentially fear-inducing way he could have done it. Nonetheless, he ordained that his people should travel that way. And it was by that fearful and awe-inspiring means that he actually saved them from their enemies and led them to the Promised Land. The situation of danger became the means of salvation. The place of threat became the place of fulfilment. Why did he do it? We do not know for certain. It was for his glory, without question. Whatever his purpose, he called his people to trust him, and he led them to walk in faith.

After years of wandering and after the adult generation who left Egypt died off (save a few exceptions), the day finally came to enter the Land of Promise and then to take the city of Jericho. It was a well-fortified city, inhabited by big strong people (giants, according to a report from the spies), and surrounded by a great wall. It is hard to imagine what it would have felt like for the Israelites to approach that city with its strong defenses, knowing the strength of the inhabitants within. Their military might was limited. By natural means they could not take the city, but God promised to give it to them. He called them to approach the walls, march around them seven times, sound the trumpet, and then simply to wait for his salvation. At any moment the enemy within could have sprung upon them or rained down an attack from above. But God brought the Israelites into that situation that his people might see his power and know his provision. The dramatic outcome is summarized so simply for us: "By faith the walls of Jericho fell down after they had been encircled for seven days" (11:30). Once again, God brought his people into frankly impossible situations, and in the midst of danger and weakness, showed them how he would achieve his saving purposes in and through those very circumstances.

Rahab

> *"By faith Rahab the prostitute did not perish with those who were disobedient, because she had given a friendly welcome to the spies."*
> *(Hebrews 11:31)*

When Joshua sent two spies into Jericho to search it out and to survey it, the spies went and lodged in the home of Rahab. The king of Jericho heard that the spies were in the midst of his city at Rahab's house, and so he demanded that she give them up. But in an act of brave and faithful defiance, she instead hid them and helped them escape, putting herself at incredible risk. Because of this act of kindness, when God brought destruction to Jericho, her household was spared. She had cast in her lot with the people of God, ultimately entrusting herself to the God of Israel. In a perilous situation, she had been given extraordinary grace to walk by faith, to stand alone in her culture and society, and to wait upon the true and living God for his salvation.

It was a fearful time and a perilous situation for this particular woman. God could have brought Rahab to himself by other means. But this was his chosen method. The story in itself is wonderful, but it takes on an added dimension of wonder when we read Jesus' genealogy in Matthew 1 and discover that Rahab the prostitute is featured in the family line of the Messiah. God not only saved this prostitute and brought her into his family through this truly fearful situation; he not only used her to bring about his saving purposes for his people to enter the Promised Land; but he used all this to prepare the way for his promised Saviour to come into the world and to bring salvation to you and to me.

MANY OTHERS

After Rahab, the writer then indicates that he has many other examples for us. He could go on and on: "And what more shall I say? For time would fail me to tell..." (11:32). He then mentions great figures of the Old Testament and of Jewish history beyond the Old Testament: Barak, Samson, Jephthah, David, Samuel, and others. He mentions kings, prophets, and individual believers of little account who, in their day, knew what it was to walk through fearful times of trial and testing, but who saw God work through those circumstances to achieve his saving purposes. These were people who put their hope in the resurrection to come (11:35) and who became people "of whom the world was not worthy" (11:38) because they lived such distinctive lives of faith.

Time would fail us too, to try and open up their stories. But Hebrews does not seem to want to linger to do that. He is simply calling them to mind to impress upon us the fact that the Old Testament is full of such stories. The history of God's people repeats this theme again and again. The writer wants to drive home the point that this is a pattern of God's activity. He often calls his people to walk through trial, and he always calls us to do so with faith. He shows us that he is powerful and faithful to use these circumstances to drive forward his saving agenda.

The message of these verses is immensely timely for us as we face our own fearful times. God has proved again and again that he can and will use times of testing and trial to move forward his plans of salvation. He has proved that those times are not incidental to his plans, interruptions to his work, or hindrances to his agenda. Far from it. Within his sovereign decrees and under his supreme power, these very things become avenues through which his saving work is accomplished. God has called his church in our generation to walk with him in faith through a fearful time and through challenging days. The trial of the coronavirus is, of course, not unique to the church (the entire global community is in this together). However, if we belong to Christ, we face this trial as believers and are called to navigate it distinctively as the people of God.

The lessons from salvation history here in Hebrews give us courage, encouragement, and hope for the days ahead. The lessons here remind us that times of trial, difficulty, danger, and even of physical risk are times not when God is absent or when his work ceases. No, these are times when God has often chosen to advance his saving agenda in remarkable and powerful ways.

In our own church, we have found that this recent time of crisis has led to a noticeable increase in hunger for God's word. As we were forced to pause in-person gatherings, many more have been joining us for our online ministries than would normally join us in person. This seems to be a widespread phenomenon, experienced by many churches in many different places. People seem to be hungry for hope, hungry for spiritual truth, hungry for the word of God. A recent op-ed appeared in the Wall Street Journal that caught my attention with its intriguing title, "A Coronavirus Great Awakening?"[1] The writer noted the impact of the Second World War on religious life in America:

---

[1] Nicholson, Robert. "A Coronavirus Great Awakening?" *Wall Street Journal*, 26 March 2020, Opinion.

> Americans, chastened by the horrors of war, turned to faith in search of truth and meaning. In the late 1940s, Gallup surveys showed more than three-quarters of Americans were members of a house of worship…Congress added the words "under God" to the Pledge of Allegiance in 1954. Some would later call this a Third Great Awakening.

The writer goes on to ask whether this contemporary crisis might have the same effect, as our society is shaken to its very core. It is a good question. Many of us are asking it. Only time will tell what lasting spiritual fruit may result.

It may be that you are reading this now because the coronavirus crisis or some other challenge has got you thinking, and you realize that you need to find hope and security beyond what this fragile world can offer. Let me encourage you: do not ignore that question. It may be that God is using a time of trial in your life to prompt you to consider where you stand before him. The offer of the gospel is for you, as it is for everyone. The Lord Jesus Christ came to address the problem of your alienation from God through dying in your place, bearing the penalty of your wrongdoing. He came to offer you forgiveness and reconciliation and life and hope, both for this life and for the life to come. Would you receive that invitation by faith, even today?

There is no doubt that the crisis facing the world in the coronavirus pandemic is lamentable and in many ways disastrous. But there is even less doubt that God is able to use such times for the sake of salvation for many. He has done it before and he can do it again. As you and I walk through times of trial, our call and our responsibility is to trust him, to walk by faith before him, and wait upon him to see what he might do. We could be discouraged in days of trial, and we might be frightened. We could be brought low. But the writer of Hebrews would urge us, and God by his word exhorts us, "let us run with endurance the race that is set before us, looking to Jesus, the founder and perfecter of our faith" (12:1-2).

Therefore, since we are surrounded by so great a cloud of witnesses, let us also lay aside every weight, and sin which clings so closely, and let us run with endurance the race that is set before us, looking to Jesus, the founder and perfecter of our faith, who for the joy that was set before him endured the cross, despising the shame, and is seated at the right hand of the throne of God.

Hebrews 12:1-2

4
Enduring in Faith

It is one thing to start a project, quite another thing to finish it. Many of us love new projects, whether it be a new work project, or a new home improvement project, or a new fitness project. There is a thrill about starting on that first morning. The second morning can feel pretty exhilarating too; the project is still fresh and the enthusiasm is still high. The third morning, well, maybe it takes the extra cup of coffee to get going, but the zeal is still there. But the fourth, the fifth morning…the second week, the third week…. Normally, over time, the sheen wears off and the energy wanes. We all know that experience. It is much easier to start just about anything than it is to finish it.

It is one thing to start the race of the Christian life. It is one thing to set off with enthusiasm following Jesus, serving him, obeying his word, and loving his people. It is quite another thing to continue running the race to the very end. If we have been following Jesus any length of time, we know the daily challenge of persevering in service and trust in the ordinary things of life. When trouble comes, when opposition appears, when suffering knocks on our door—when our world is shaken by a pandemic, perhaps—the challenge can actually seem quite beyond us.

Here at the opening of chapter 12, Hebrews paints for us a vivid picture of the Christian life. He takes us to a great stadium with a long race track, and he invites us to imagine ourselves as runners on the track, enduring a long and grueling race. This is no mere sprint, but a full-length marathon. The sun is hot above us, our legs are feeling the strain, our chest is tight with exertion. Jesus is at the finish line, and we still have some distance to cover. What will it take to keep going?

The two opening verses of Hebrews 12 really cap off the great lessons of chapter 11 (hence their inclusion here in a study focused on that chapter). As we have noticed before, this broader section began at the end of chapter 10 with a call to endure:

> For you have need of endurance, so that when you have done the will of God you may receive what is promised. For, "Yet a little while, and the coming one will come and will not delay; but my righteous one shall live by faith, and if he shrinks back, my soul has no pleasure in him." (Hebrews 10:36-38, citing Habakkuk 2:3-4)

The writer wants to call us and help us to endure to the end, living by faith. All the wonderful models of faith in chapter 11 were there to help us do this very thing. Now here at the start of chapter 12 comes a summary call, encouragement, and exhortation. Within it, I think we are given three key insights for enduring in faith.

How do we run the race to the end? *We listen to the witnesses, we lay aside all weight, and we look to Jesus.*

Listen to the Witnesses

> *"Therefore, since we are surrounded by so great a cloud of witnesses..." (Hebrews 12:1)*

To run the race to the end, we listen to the witnesses that have gone before. In a sense, this mention of the witnesses is a matter of preamble and background to the central call to run the race with endurance that is coming at the end of verse 1. Nonetheless, the mention of the witnesses is significant here. The writer is telling us that the stories and testimonies of these witnesses, who are the heroes of faith of chapter 11, are key for us if we are to keep going.

I have to say, one person I do not envy at the present time is the Canadian prime minister. Leadership is always hard, but leadership in times of crisis is especially daunting. Even on a good day, that level of leadership must be quite lonely. There is only one prime minister of any given country at any given time, and so the number of people who would appreciate exactly the challenges and pressures that the prime minister faces are very few. I have always appreciated the fact that, in the main corridor on the west side of the centre block of Parliament, the walls are lined with portraits of former prime ministers. It is quite interesting to study those portraits and get a bit of a sense of those leaders. I imagine that it does the current prime minister good to walk down that corridor, to notice those portraits, and to remember the stories of those leaders who have gone before. It must do him good to consider what it must have been like for Sir Robert Borden to lead the nation through the First World War, or for William Lyon Mackenzie King to lead through the Second World War. When things seem hard and when crisis strikes, remembering the stories of those who have gone before must be of some help. In times of difficulty, walking through that gallery must bring encouragement to endure.

Hebrews has just led us through a great gallery of believers of old who lived the life of faith, often in tremendously hard times and often in the face of potentially overwhelming obstacles. Remember some of the things we have been told of these believers of old:

> They were stoned, they were sawn in two, they were killed with the sword. They went about in skins of sheep and goats, destitute, afflicted, mistreated—of whom the world was not worthy—wandering about in deserts and mountains, and in dens and caves of the earth. (Hebrews 11:37-38)

We can be a little perplexed when the writer refers to the believers of old as "a cloud of witnesses" (12:1). Is he talking about believers of old who perhaps witness our earthly race from heaven above? Such an idea is intriguing, but does not have much other support in the Bible. In the original Greek, just like in English, a "witness" can either be someone who watches something (a witness of an event, maybe a crime), or it can be someone who bears testimony about something. We often talk of Christians as those who witness to the truth of the gospel and to the person of Jesus Christ. When we use the term in that way, we mean that such people have something to say about Jesus to the wider world. We have just spent the whole of chapter 11 hearing the stories of these believers of old, listening to their testimony of faith. It seems quite clear that here in verse 1 the focus is on these Old Testament believers as those who witness to God's faithfulness as they trust in him. The point does not seem to be that they are observing our race (even though we will meet them at the finish line in heaven), but rather that they have a story to tell us and an experience to relate to us. Hebrews reminds us that we run our Christian race, as it were, along a track surrounded by portraits—stories and testimonies—of those who have gone before us and who have now arrived safely at the destination.

We certainly need to hear their stories and listen to their testimonies of faith. Hebrews 11 is such a rich chapter for us because it crystalizes some of the most outstanding testimonies of faith from the Old Testament. But we need to look beyond just Hebrews 11. We need to be those who immerse ourselves in the stories of the Bible to observe how these believers of old lived as followers of the Lord. Of course, we need to read our Bibles and develop our Christian worldview and our biblical theology and see how all the stories of the Old Testament point to Christ. We need to read the Old Testament with all those theological lenses on, asking all those important questions. But at the same time, we need to do the very simple thing of listening to the stories, observing the people within the stories, and learning (from the godly ones, at least!) what it looks like to live day-by-day as God's people, through all the ups-and-downs of life.

There is a danger that our reading and study of the Bible can become rather impoverished if we always look for the "deeper things," but forget simply to observe and learn from these testimonies of faith. All of us need to take care that we do not overlook these stories. There is an important challenge for parents in this. When you teach your children the Scriptures, be careful not to ignore the stories and character studies in favour of getting directly to theological teaching points. Our children need to know the shape of those stories to have a rounded understanding of the basic character of the life of faith. Times have changed since the books of the Bible were written; our contexts are very different; but the human heart is just the same, and God has not changed at all. So the lessons of these testimonies are ever fresh and relevant. In seasons of trial, it is such a help to go back and read the story of Abraham, of David, or of Daniel, and to remember that God's people have faced plenty of difficulty before us. God has been gracious to pick them up when they have stumbled, to sustain them when it seemed like they might faint on the way, and to give them the faith they needed to endure. As we look at them and hear their stories afresh, we are helped by the Spirit of God to think, "Yes, by his grace, I can keep going."

LAY ASIDE EVERY WEIGHT

> *"Therefore, since we are surrounded by so great a cloud of witnesses, let us also lay aside every weight, and sin which clings so closely..." (Hebrews 12:1)*

When you want to go the distance, it is important to travel light. Near our home in Ottawa there is an aviation museum that holds an outstanding collection of heritage aircraft. All planes are fascinating to me, but some of the very earliest aircraft in the collection tend to catch my attention—not because they are especially beautiful or sophisticated, but actually because they are so very basic. It is easy to feel a little nervous just looking at some of them. It is remarkable to think that people entrusted their lives to the early bi-planes that were so very flimsy. The early planes were characterized, perhaps above all else, by the extremes to which their designers went in order to reduce weight. A number of the very early planes in this particular collection actually have wings that are covered, not by metal or wood, but by canvas. To make the plane fly, and to allow it to cover distance, every weight was set aside, cut down, and reduced.

If you have ever gone on a hiking expedition, perhaps in the Rocky Mountains, or if you have ever embarked on a long canoe trip, perhaps in the wilds of northern Ontario, you will know something about packing light. I remember going on a ten-day canoe trip as a teenager. Before we went we had to gather everything we planned to carry, and we had to demonstrate to the expedition leaders that every single item would fit in our backpack. Nothing extra could come. It seemed a tough discipline at the outset, but we would later be grateful for it.

The Christian life involves a great pilgrimage, a challenging journey. To return to the imagery of the race-track, it is a marathon and not a sprint. We are called to go the distance: day-by-day, week-by-week, month-by-month, year-by-year, decade-by-decade, until the Lord takes us home. We need to be so very careful that we lay aside anything that will slow us down. For the saints of old in chapter 11, they had to make some hard decisions about the things they would carry with them and the things they would set aside. They had to make some hard decisions about the things they would value and the things they would not. Abraham had to let go of his hold on his parents' homeland. Moses had to set aside the treasures of Egypt and the privileges of the royal household. For us today, there may be some things in this world—some dreams, priorities, treasures, or attachments—that are not necessarily wrong in themselves, but that slow us down in the Christian race.

Maybe for you, it is career ambition. There is nothing wrong about your job in and of itself, but ambition fills your heart and consumes your attention in such a way that your Christian growth is stunted. Your time to serve, your time in the word, and your ability to pray are all limited, and you know it. And so, just maybe, ambition is a weight that needs to be set aside. Or maybe for you it is your sport commitments. You play on teams, have talent, and you love it. But practices, games, and tournaments take evenings and weekends and intrude on Sundays. The sport itself is wholesome, but the commitment is stunting your growth and slowing you down. Or maybe for you it is your pass-times and hobbies, or diversions like Facebook, Netflix, and Spotify. They may not be all bad in themselves, but as you look at the time and energy you invest in them, you see they are a weight in your Christian race, slowing you down. You see that something needs to change. Or maybe for you it is your possessions. You just have too much stuff. Paying for it and caring for it is consuming all your energy and attention. None of it is necessarily evil in itself. But the effect on your Christian life is to slow you down, to stunt your growth, and to limit your service of Christ. And maybe something just has to go. What are the commitments and attachments in your life that the Lord might be calling you to re-evaluate, to reduce in some way, to cut out so that you will be less weighed down in your Christian race?

The coronavirus pandemic has forced us to think about death more than we want to as a society. But, of course, it is actually healthy for us to think about death from time to time.

Thinking about death forces us to consider our fundamental priorities and what matters most to us in life, in the final accounting. For the Christian, when we reach our deathbed, we know that the thing that will matter most is this: Have I run the race well; have I endured in faithfulness to the end? We want to hear those all-important words from the Master, "Well done, good and faithful servant" (Matthew 25:21). We will not care much about the possessions we have accumulated, the accolades we have gathered, or the career we have built. We will care simply that we have run, and run well, the race of faith. What weights do you need to set aside to make it to the end?

We need to lay aside those general weights. But then more specifically, we need to lay aside "the sin which clings so closely" (Hebrews 12:1). If the first part of the image of 12:1 speaks of a runner needing to make sure he is travelling as light as possible, this next part of the image speaks to the need to make sure his legs and ankles are not getting caught up in the weeds and the brush at the side of the track. If you are not running your Christian race on a clear track, but veering into the brambles, you are going to get slowed down, tripped up, waylaid on the journey. If we have been Christians for any time at all, we all know the danger of the sin which clings so closely, the weeds that will wrap their way around our ankles and hold us back and drag us down. None of us ever reaches the point in the Christian life where sin stops being a problem for us, when temptation is no longer an issue. If you think you are there, watch out, because you are under a delusion, and you will let your guard down. Even though we are made new in Christ, our sinful nature, our flesh, is still there. We are not freed from that old nature until the day we die. We have an ongoing battle with sin, as the sinful nature resists the work of the Spirit of Christ within us (see, for example, Romans 6:12, 1 Peter 2:11). With the help of the Spirit, we have a role to play in this battle. We need to prayerfully, dependently, and energetically lay aside the sin which so easily entangles us in the race.

We all know what it is to be tripped up by sin. Frankly, we all know what it is to allow ourselves to run too near to the edge of the track, too close to the encroaching weeds. We know what it is to allow ourselves to become entangled. Sometimes we are tripped up by surprise. But often, as we look back, we recognize that we have allowed ourselves to drift to the edge of the track and to embrace risk. Where are the particular areas of risk, of temptation, in your life? With a moment or two of honest reflection, each one of us knows where those weeds are lining the track of our own Christian life. What are the sins you need to lay aside, the weeds and brambles you need to be more careful to avoid? What steps can you take, even today, to do that? Hebrews says to us, quite simply: Lay them aside. Cut them down. Step away from them. Do not let them entangle you. The constant danger is that they might slow you down, trip you up, and ruin your race.

Look to Jesus

> *"...looking to Jesus, the founder and perfecter of our faith, who for the joy that was set before him endured the cross, despising the shame, and is seated at the right hand of the throne of God."*
> *(Hebrews 12:2)*

We do not need to be experts on running marathons to know that if we see a runner looking at his feet or a runner looking back at where she has come from, we are seeing a runner who is in trouble, a runner who has lost focus, a runner who has probably lost hope. In a great race, every runner who means to finish looks ahead to the goal. In our Christian race, Jesus is our all-in-all. He is the coach who put us on the track; he is the pacesetter for the race; he is the forerunner who has reached the finish line before us; he is the enabler who strengthens us to run; and he is himself the goal of our race. Hebrews puts it so richly: he is the "founder" and the "perfecter" of our faith. He is himself the basis of our faith: in his life and death and resurrection, he did everything to enable us to come to the Father. He not only achieves our salvation in that way, but he completes his saving work in us, transforming us into his image, keeping us by his Spirit right to the end. He is our everything in the race.

As we look to him, we have our eyes fixed on the one who ran this race and who finished this race, and who did so perfectly. As he lived his earthly life, even though he is God the Son, he had to trust the Father each day, and he had to learn to obey the Father through many trials. We catch a profound glimpse of this in Hebrews 5:7-8:

> In the days of his flesh, Jesus offered up prayers and supplications, with loud cries and tears, to him who was able to save him from death, and he was heard because of his reverence. Although he was a son, he learned obedience through what he suffered.

Hebrews tells us that, in the deepest of those trials, at the cross itself, Jesus endured by looking to the joy that was set before him. He endured by looking forward to his arrival at his heavenly home, to being with the Father and sitting at his right hand on high. The prospect of that joyful day kept him going.

More than that, it enabled him to "despise the shame" of the cross (12:2). The cross was designed not only to torture but to humiliate the sufferer who was put on gruesome public display. But rather than be crushed by this experience of shame, Jesus was enabled to despise it. He did that because he had his eyes fixed on the future. Yes, there is suffering now, but glory is coming. Yes, this seems shameful to the watching world. But the cross was part of the set path that Jesus would travel to receive his crown. The cross was actually the way to glory. Jesus knew that, before long, he would be seated at the right hand of the throne of God on high. And so, because of all this, Jesus persevered and endured.

If we are going to go the distance in the Christian life, if we are going to persevere when times are hard, if we are going to keep trusting Jesus and walking with him through pandemic and grief and financial difficulties and disruptions to life and all the rest, we are going to have to fix our eyes on Jesus. We are going to have to set the gaze of our heart upon the future that we will enjoy with him when we gather in his immediate presence, and delight in his goodness. How eagerly and earnestly are you looking to Jesus where he is seated in glory above? How much do you look forward to the day when we will see him face-to-face? How real are these things to you, and how precious?

In normal times, when the world is running as it usually does, when our activities, distractions, and recreations are uninhibited by crisis or pandemic, it is easy for us to be distracted by the pleasures and pursuits of this world. It is easy for us, frankly, to be too satisfied by those things. But times of crisis give us an unusual opportunity to fix our eyes on Jesus and our heavenly home. You may know this simple old chorus, which seems particularly relevant to the present time: "Turn your eyes upon Jesus, look full in his wonderful face, and the things of earth will grow strangely dim, in the light of his glory and grace."[2] There is a sense in which, for all of us, the things of earth have grown a little less bright—*a little more dim*—in the days of the pandemic. We have been unable to see and experience all the things of this world as we normally would. At the same time, we are seeing with a fresh clarity how fragile they are, how passing and temporary. That is a valuable insight, and the crisis has provided an enforced opportunity to learn it afresh. But as we grapple with the dimness of this present world, we need to fix our eyes on the Lord Jesus and see the brightness of his glory and grace. That is what gives us hope and joy and spiritual energy for persevering in faith in turbulent days.

How, then, do we look to Jesus? The writer is not saying that we should simply close our eyes and imagine what Jesus looks like. He is not suggesting that we should gaze up into the clouds in the hope of catching a glimpse of his heavenly court. Surely we look to Jesus as he has revealed himself to us in his word. We look to the pages of Scripture and we observe his work, we hear his voice, and we see him with the eyes of faith. Doing this, however, requires care and effort. It requires us to make space in our days and in the scope of our mind's attention to quieten ourselves, set aside distraction, and open his word. It requires self-discipline and a heart that longs to see him. But we need to see him by faith day-by-day if we are going to endure in this race. He is the one who can enable us to finish, and he will surely do that as we look to him.

---

[2] Helen H. Lemmel, "Turn your eyes upon Jesus."

Living by Faith

    The Christian life is a marathon and not a sprint. Any marathon runner will tell you that finishing a race takes discipline and endurance. We need all the help we can get in this. So, how do we endure? We listen to the witnesses; we lay aside every weight that might slow us down; and we look to Jesus, who founded our faith by his saving work, who will finish his work in us by his Spirit, and who models for us that perfect faithful endurance to the end.

Conclusion

The great gallery of faith in Hebrews 11 stands not as a tribute to the believers of old so much as a testimony to the faithfulness of the God they trusted and served. They walked through their own seasons of uncertainty, danger, and opposition, and the Lord upheld each one of them in faith. Hebrews reminds us that "Jesus Christ is the same yesterday and today and forever" (Hebrews 13:8). It is my hope and prayer that you will be enabled to trust him, whatever may come in the days ahead.

If you have read this book as an onlooker and enquirer, may I close by encouraging you—*and urging you*—to come by faith to this trustworthy and gracious God. He invites us to approach him, not because we have any right to claim his welcome or his kindness, but because he gave his Son to die for our failures and our wrongdoing, and to rise again in victory over death. Hebrews does not gloss over the sobering realities of life in this world, but offers hope in Jesus to all who come to him in repentance and faith:

> And just as it is appointed for man to die once, and after that comes judgment, so Christ, having been offered once to bear the sins of many, will appear a second time, not to deal with sin but to save those who are eagerly waiting for him. (Hebrews 9:27–28)

About the Author

Jonathan Griffiths serves as Lead Pastor of the Metropolitan Bible Church in Ottawa, Canada. He studied theology at the University of Oxford and completed his PhD on the book of Hebrews at the University of Cambridge. He is the author of a number of books, most recently, *Preaching in the New Testament* (IVP, 2017).

Scripture Index

Old Testament

Genesis
- 4:1–5 7
- 5:21 11
- 6:5–8 14
- 12:1 21
- 12:4 21
- 48:16 30
- 50:24–25 31

Exodus
- 2:1 38
- 2:2 38

Habakkuk
- 2:3–4 .... 2, 37, 53

New Testament

Matthew
  1:2 27
  16:17-19 32
  25:21 60
John
  1:29 7
Romans
  6:1 61
  6:12 61
Ephesians
  1:18-20 30
2 Timothy
  2:9 33
Hebrews
  9:27-28 67
  10:36-38 53
  11:1 ....1, 19
  11:4 6
  11:5 10
  11:7 13
  11:8 21
  11:11 27
  11:21 30
  11:23 .... 35, 37
  11:24 40
  11:26 40
  11:29 44
  11:30 46
  11:13-16 23
  11:1-7 1
  11:23-40 35
  11:37-38 55
  11:8-22 2
  11:9-10 22
  12:1 .... 54, 57, 60
  12:2 62
  12:1-2 51
  13:8 67
James
  4:13-17 19
2 Peter
  3:1-13 15

Date Completed	Name

H&E Publications

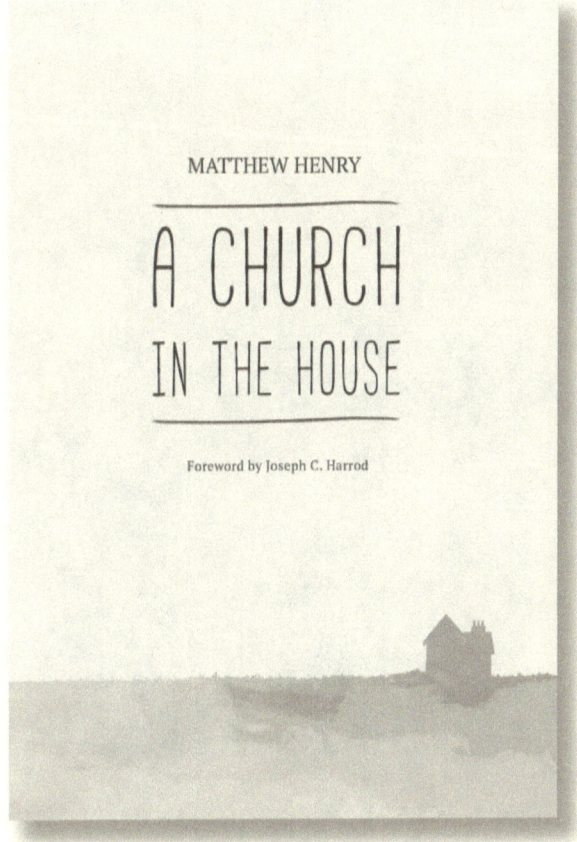

ISBN: 978-1-77526-333-3

Matthew Henry exhorts fathers to lead their homes well in family worship. This is an excellent resource for those who are aiming to be faithful in family discipleship.

ISBN: 978-1-77526-334-0

Fuller deals with the issue of backsliding: when genuine Christians lose their passion for Christ and his kingdom. This was not a theoretical issue for Fuller, therefore, and his words, weighty when he first wrote them, are still worthy of being pondered—and acted upon.

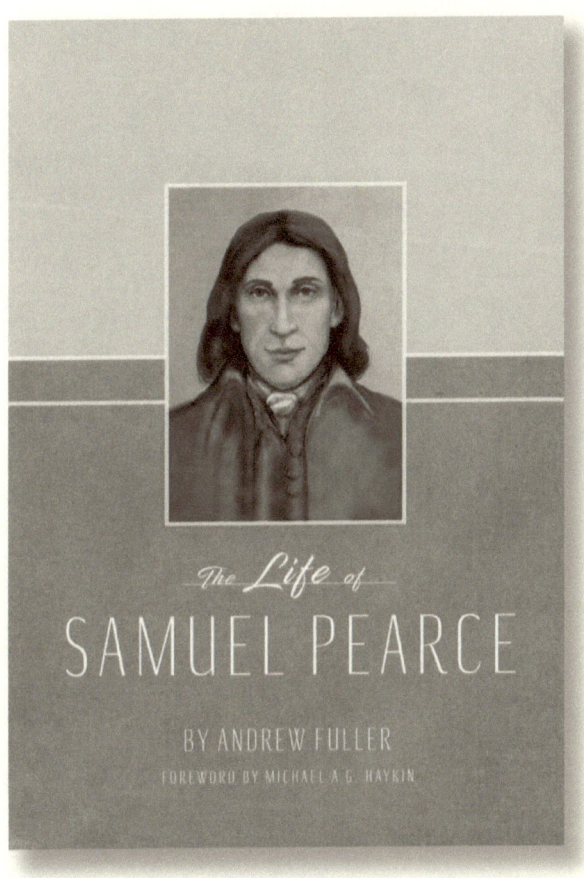

ISBN: 978-1-77526-339-5

In the eyes of Fuller, Samuel Pearce (1766–1799) was the epitome of the spirituality of their community. In fact, in that far-off day of the late eighteenth century Pearce was indeed well known for the anointing that attended his preaching and for the depth of his spirituality. It was said of him that "his ardour … gave him a kind of ubiquity; as a man and a preacher, he was known, he was felt everywhere."

Notes

Notes

Notes

Notes

Notes

Notes

Notes

Notes

H&E Publishing
www.HesedAndEmet.com

www.ingramcontent.com/pod-product-compliance
Lightning Source LLC
Chambersburg PA
CBHW020544080526
44583CB00013B/979